British Library Cataloguing in Publication Data
Wood, Jakki
By the canal.
1. Great Britain. Canals
I. Title II. Series
386'.46'0941

ISBN 0-340-50232-0

Text and illustrations copyright © Jacqueline Wood 1989

First published 1989

Published by Hodder and Stoughton Children's Books,
a division of Hodder and Stoughton Ltd
Mill Road, Dunton Green, Sevenoaks Kent TN13 2YA

Printed in Belgium by Proost International Book Production

All rights reserved

By the Canal

by Jakki Wood

Judy　　Alex　Dad　Peter　Sam　Sam's Dad

HODDER AND STOUGHTON
LONDON SYDNEY AUCKLAND TORONTO

Peter and Judy like rainy days, even in summer. The canal towpaths are lovely and muddy. There are plenty of puddles to splash through.

'Look at those ducks,' says Alex.

◄ Reedmace

◄ Water horsetail

Mallards are common wild ducks. When you see them 'up-ending', they are looking for food.

The white patch on a coot's forehead is bare skin. This is why we say 'as bald as a coot'. Young coots have a bright red head.

Alex and Peter watch dragonflies skim across the water. Judy barks at a rabbit, which dashes through the long grass into a bramble bush.

'You naughty girl,' shouts Peter. 'You've frightened that rabbit.'

A mayfly is on the flowering-rush. The plant is just in bud. A mayfly lives for about four days, having spent a year underwater as a nymph.

Dragonfly and damselfly nymphs also spend a year or more underwater before emerging as adults.

Large red damselfly

Banded damselfly

Giant dragonfly

◀ *Flowering-rush*

◀ *Mayfly*

Judy sniffs at the bush until Alex pulls her back onto the path.

'Now look. You're covered in bits of grass.'

It looks as if Judy is covered in grass seeds, but in fact no seeds have formed yet. The grasses are still flowering. Judy has lots of anthers stuck to her. Anthers are the part of a flower which contain pollen.

stigma
filaments
anthers
pollen

Timothy grass

Cock's-foot

Ribwort plantain

Dandelion

◄ Cinnabar moth
▼ Red clover

A long, narrow boat is tied up by the lock. Inside, a black bull terrier barks at Judy. Judy barks back.

'What a noise!' says Peter.

This wooden narrow boat used to carry cargoes of coal and grain. Now it is used by holiday-makers.

The narrow boat is painted with traditional roses and castles on the cabin door and sides, on the water cans, and on the cabin roof.

'Peter, someone lives on that boat. Don't be so nosy.'
'Come and look,' Peter replies. 'It's really old-fashioned inside.'

Years ago, a whole family lived and slept in this tiny cabin. Everything had to be kept neat and tidy. You can see the cooking pots and copper kettle in their place on the stove.

The narrow boat didn't have electricity. Instead, the family used oil for lighting and heat. Water was stored in cans on the cabin roof.

Farther along the bank Peter meets his friend Sam.

'Look how many fish my dad's caught,' says Sam proudly. 'And look at my sticklebacks.'

In spring, the male stickleback is bright red in order to attract females to the nest he is building on the canal bottom. A stickleback's spines prevent it from being swallowed by a bigger fish.

Great diving beetle

Pond snail

Stickleback

Roach

Tench

◀ Rudd

Sam's dad points to a pair of moorhens, which have built their untidy nest in a yellow flag plant growing in the water.

'Look! Those tiny chicks can already swim.'

▲ Alder tree with woody cones from last autumn, and new ripening cones

Yellow flag

Caddis-fly

Water snail

Moorhen chicks have red beaks and bright blue eye patches. They can swim immediately after hatching.

Caddis-flies live for only a few days. They are most active at dusk.

The narrow boat is going through the lock. The children help to open the lock gates.

'Push, Alex, push,' shouts Peter.

'I am pushing,' says Alex. 'Where's Judy gone?'

If a river or canal is flowing fast downhill, boats find it difficult to steer against the current. By making locks (which are rather like stairs), long stretches of water can be kept level and slow-flowing.

The longest chain of locks, thirty in all, can be found at Tardebrigge, on the Worcester and Birmingham Canal.

1 *A boat approaches a lock gate. The paddles in the gate are opened and the water level between the lock gates rises.*

2 *When water levels are equal, paddles are closed and the first lock gate is opened. The boat enters the lock.*

3 *When the boat is in the lock, both gates are shut and the paddles in the second gate are opened to let the water out.*

4 *When the water levels are the same, the second lock gates are opened and the boat goes on its way.*

'Judy! Judy!' Peter's voice echoes down the tunnel. The tunnel tow-path is wide enough for a horse to walk along. Horses were once used to pull narrow boats.

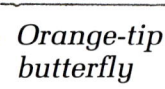
Orange-tip butterfly

Small Tortoiseshell butterfly

Swallows swoop down to catch gnats emerging from the water. Butterflies sun themselves on the warm brickwork. A drone-fly hovers near the ragged-robin flowers. It looks and sounds just like a male (drone) honey-bee.

There are lots of different flowers growing along the bank. Peter wants to take a bunch home.

'No,' says Dad. 'You shouldn't pick wild flowers.'

The leaves of the water-crowfoot are shaped differently above and below the water line.

Caddis-fly larvae build protective cases of leaves, pebbles, bark, or snails' shells around themselves.

Water-boatman

Whirligig beetle

Great pond snail

Dragonfly nymph

Stickleback's nest

Mayfly nymph

Canadian pondweed ▼

Caddis-fly larvae ▼

'Don't go near the edge, Peter,' warns Alex. 'Come away, Judy! You mustn't drink that dirty water.'

'No, you might swallow a fish,' laughs Peter.

It starts to rain again.

'Look at the patterns the rain makes on the water,' says Alex. Peter picks up a huge leaf to use as an umbrella.

'Let's go home before we get soaked.'

Large butterbur leaves form cool, damp, dark places for frogs and toads, like this common toad, to shelter in.

Toads start their lives as tadpoles, but as they grow up they are able to live on land, too. They hide during the day in damp corners of fields and gardens, coming out at night to hunt for worms and grubs. They hibernate during the winter.

INDEX

alder tree 15

beetles 7, 13, 22
birds 2, 3, 14, 15, 18
bramble bush 4, 5
butterbur 25
butterflies 18, 21

Cabbage White butterfly 21
caddis-fly 15, 22
campion, red, white 21
Canadian pondweed 22
Cinnabar moth 7
cock's-foot 7
comfrey 21
coot 3
cow parsley 21

damselfly, banded, large red 5

dandelion 7
dragonfly, giant 4, 5
dragonfly nymph 22
dronefly 18
ducks 2, 3

fish 13, 23
flowering-rush 5
flowers 7, 14, 15, 18
foxglove 21

gnat 18
grasses 6, 7
great diving beetle 13

locks 16, 17

mallard 3
mayfly 5, 6, 22
moorhens 14, 15
moth 7